TIME FOR KIDS®

BEGINNING **1** READER · *Science Scoops*

Plants!

By the Editors of TIME For Kids
WITH BRENDA IASEVOLI

HarperCollinsPublishers

About the Author: Brenda Iasevoli has worked as a fourth-grade teacher, a writer, and an editor. As a teacher, she enjoyed watching students grow and learn. As an editor at TIME For Kids®, she relishes writing about topics that she might not have learned about otherwise. Brenda Iasevoli is also the author of the TIME For Kids® Science Scoops book ANTS!

To Nathan, a plant's best friend.

Special thanks to Park Ranger James Wheeler of the Redwood National and State Parks in California and Marie Long, the reference librarian at the LuEsther T. Mertz Library in The New York Botanical Garden. —B.I.

Library of Congress Cataloging-in-Publication Data is available.

ISBN-10: 0-06-078218-8 (pbk.) — ISBN-10: 0-06-078219-6 (trade)
ISBN-13: 978-0-06-078218-4 (pbk.) — ISBN-13: 978-0-06-078219-1 (trade)

1 2 3 4 5 6 7 8 9 10
First Edition

Copyright © by Time Inc.
TIME FOR KIDS and the Red Border Design are Trademarks of Time Inc. used under license.

Photography and Illustration Credits:
Cover: Kevin Schafer; cover inset: Neil Lucas—naturepl.com; cover front flap: Gregory Ochocki—Photo Researchers; title page: Carr Clifton—Minden; pg. 3: M. Loup—Peter Arnold; pp. 4–5: David Tipling—naturepl.com; pp. 6–7: Michael & Patricia Fogden—Minden; pp. 8–9: Runk/Schoenberger/Grant Heilman (2); pp. 10–11: Barry Runk/Stan/Grant Heilman (2); pp. 12-13: Jean Robert—Lonely Planet Images; pp. 14–15: Brad Wrobleski—Masterfile; pp. 16–17: Philippe Bayle—Peter Arnold Inc.; pp. 18–19: Barry Runk/Stan/Grant Heilman; pp. 20–21: Mark Moffett—Minden; pp. 22–23: Frank Krahmer—ImageState/Alamy; pp. 24–25: Ed Reschke—Peter Arnold; pg. 25 (inset): Barbara Spurll; pp. 26–27: Dennis MacDonald—PhotoEdit; pp. 28–29: William A. Blake—Corbis; pg. 28 (inset): John Courtney; pp. 30-31: Lynda Richardson—Corbis; pg. 32 (habitat): Jean Robert—Lonely Planet Images; pg. 32 (leaves): Ed Reschke—Peter Arnold; pg. 32 (pollen): Michael & Patricia Fogden—Minden; pg. 32 (roots): Runk/Stan/Grant Heilman; pg. 32 (seed): Runk/Schoenberger/Grant Heilman; pg. 32 (stem): Runk/Stan/Grant Heilman.

Acknowledgments:
For TIME FOR KIDS: Editorial Director: Keith Garton; Editor: Nelida Gonzalez Cutler; Art Director: Rachel Smith; Photography Editor: Jill Tatara

 Check us out at www.timeforkids.com

What grows at the top of
a mountain?
What grows at the bottom
of an ocean?
Plants!

Plants can be small or big. Grass and trees are plants. Some plants have flowers.

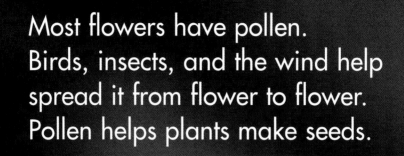

Most flowers have pollen.
Birds, insects, and the wind help
spread it from flower to flower.
Pollen helps plants make seeds.

Most plants grow from a seed.

The seed takes in minerals
and water through the root.

The stem carries minerals and water to the leaves. Plants need water to grow.

Many plants live in the rainforest. The warm, wet habitat is perfect for them.

But plants can also grow
in the dry, hot desert.
The cactus stores water
inside its stems and leaves.

Plants need food to grow.
Some plants make their own.
They use water, air, and sunlight
to make food.

Some plants catch their food.
The leaves of the Venus flytrap
hold a sweet juice.
When an insect tries to sip it,
the leaves snap shut.

Some plants and insects
help each other.
Ants sting animals that
eat acacia trees.
The trees give the ants
food and shelter.

A few plants steal food.
This strangler fig tree wraps
itself around a palm tree.
It eats the palm tree's food.

Do not touch poison ivy!
Its three shiny leaves contain oil.
The oil can cause an itchy, red rash.

That Is Amazing!

Do not get too close to the
rafflesia plant!
Its giant flower smells of
rotting meat.
This flower is the
biggest in the world.
It can be three
feet wide.

There are more than 300,000 types of plants.
Some plants give us fruit to eat.

That Is Amazing!

Redwood trees grow in California. They are the world's tallest plants. These trees can be three hundred fifty feet tall. That's taller than the Statue of Liberty!

We need plants.
They make clean air
for us to breathe.

Be a friend to plants. We could not live without them!

WORDS  to Know

Habitat: the area in which an animal or plant lives

Roots: the parts of a plant that take in minerals and water

Leaves: the flat parts of a plant growing from a stem

Seed: a plant part that contains the beginning of a new plant

Pollen: tiny, powdery grains from flowers that help make seeds

Stem: the part of a plant that carries water and food from the roots to the leaves